PAUL McCARTNEY

Songs for Linda

My Love · Calico Skies · Golden Earth Girl
Warm and Beautiful · Somedays · She's My Baby

FOR STRING QUARTET

VIOLIN 1

FABER *ff* MUSIC

IN ASSOCIATION WITH MPL COMMUNICATIONS

Recorded by the Loma Mar Quartet on the EMI CD 'Working Classical' (7243 5 56897 2 6)

Durations: each 2–3 minutes

Set of parts ISBN 0-571-52086-3

Score available separately ISBN 0-571-52093-6

Also available:

Paul McCartney: *Haymakers* and *Midwife* for string quartet
Score ISBN 0-571-52030-8
Set of parts ISBN 0-571-52040-5

My Love

PAUL McCARTNEY
Arr. Michael Thomas and
The Loma Mar Quartet

Violin I

Calico Skies

PAUL McCARTNEY
Arr. The Loma Mar Quartet

♩. = 56

mf

8

16

24 **A** *p*

mf

33 **B**

f

41

mf

48 **C**

mp

56

p

mf

64

73

cresc.

p *sub.*

82 **D**

pp

mp

89

poco rit.

dim.

PAUL McCARTNEY
Songs for Linda

My Love · Calico Skies · Golden Earth Girl
Warm and Beautiful · Somedays · She's My Baby

FOR STRING QUARTET

VIOLA

FABER ***ff*** MUSIC

IN ASSOCIATION WITH MPL COMMUNICATIONS

Recorded by the Loma Mar Quartet on the EMI CD 'Working Classical' (7243 5 56897 2 6)

Durations: each 2–3 minutes

Set of parts ISBN 0-571-52086-3

Score available separately ISBN 0-571-52093-6

Also available:

Paul McCartney: *Haymakers* and *Midwife* for string quartet
Score ISBN 0-571-52030-8
Set of parts ISBN 0-571-52040-5

My Love

PAUL McCARTNEY
Arr. Michael Thomas and
The Loma Mar Quartet

Viola
Calico Skies

PAUL McCARTNEY
Arr. The Loma Mar Quartet

Golden Earth Girl

PAUL McCARTNEY
Arr. The Loma Mar Quartet

6

Viola

Warm and Beautiful

PAUL McCARTNEY
Arr. Michael Thomas and
The Loma Mar Quartet

© 2001 by MPL Communications Ltd.

Somedays

PAUL McCARTNEY
Arr. The Loma Mar Quartet

© 2001 by MPL Communications Ltd.

Viola

She's My Baby

PAUL McCARTNEY
Arr. Robert Pansera and
The Loma Mar Quartet

PAUL McCARTNEY
Songs for Linda

My Love · Calico Skies · Golden Earth Girl
Warm and Beautiful · Somedays · She's My Baby

FOR STRING QUARTET

CELLO

FABER *ff* MUSIC

IN ASSOCIATION WITH MPL COMMUNICATIONS

Recorded by the Loma Mar Quartet on the EMI CD 'Working Classical' (7243 5 56897 2 6)

Durations: each 2–3 minutes

Set of parts ISBN 0-571-52086-3

Score available separately ISBN 0-571-52093-6

Also available:

Paul McCartney: *Haymakers* and *Midwife* for string quartet
Score ISBN 0-571-52030-8
Set of parts ISBN 0-571-52040-5

My Love

PAUL McCARTNEY
Arr. Michael Thomas and
The Loma Mar Quartet

Violoncello

Calico Skies

PAUL McCARTNEY
Arr. The Loma Mar Quartet

Golden Earth Girl

PAUL McCARTNEY
Arr. The Loma Mar Quartet

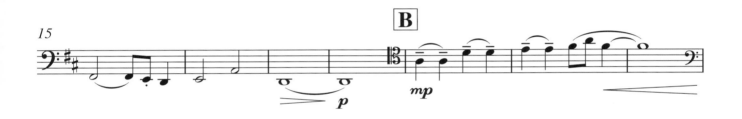

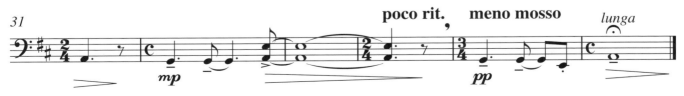

Warm and Beautiful

PAUL McCARTNEY
Arr. Michael Thomas and
The Loma Mar Quartet

Somedays

PAUL McCARTNEY
Arr. The Loma Mar Quartet

Violoncello

She's My Baby

PAUL McCARTNEY
Arr. Robert Pansera and
The Loma Mar Quartet

PAUL McCARTNEY
Songs for Linda

My Love · Calico Skies · Golden Earth Girl
Warm and Beautiful · Somedays · She's My Baby

FOR STRING QUARTET

VIOLIN 2

FABER *ff* MUSIC

IN ASSOCIATION WITH MPL COMMUNICATIONS

Recorded by the Loma Mar Quartet on the EMI CD 'Working Classical' (7243 5 56897 2 6)

Durations: each 2–3 minutes

Set of parts ISBN 0-571-52086-3

Score available separately ISBN 0-571-52093-6

Also available:

Paul McCartney: *Haymakers* and *Midwife* for string quartet
Score ISBN 0-571-52030-8
Set of parts ISBN 0-571-52040-5

My Love

PAUL McCARTNEY
Arr. Michael Thomas and
The Loma Mar Quartet

Violin II

Calico Skies

PAUL McCARTNEY
Arr. The Loma Mar Quartet

Golden Earth Girl

PAUL McCARTNEY
Arr. The Loma Mar Quartet

Warm and Beautiful

PAUL McCARTNEY
Arr. Michael Thomas and
The Loma Mar Quartet

Somedays

PAUL McCARTNEY
Arr. The Loma Mar Quartet

She's My Baby

PAUL McCARTNEY
Arr. Robert Pansera and
The Loma Mar Quartet

Golden Earth Girl

PAUL McCARTNEY
Arr. The Loma Mar Quartet

Warm and Beautiful

PAUL McCARTNEY
Arr. Michael Thomas and
The Loma Mar Quartet

Somedays

PAUL McCARTNEY
Arr. The Loma Mar Quartet

Violin I
She's My Baby

PAUL McCARTNEY
Arr. Robert Pansera and
The Loma Mar Quartet